D1716360

For Kathy Kaperick

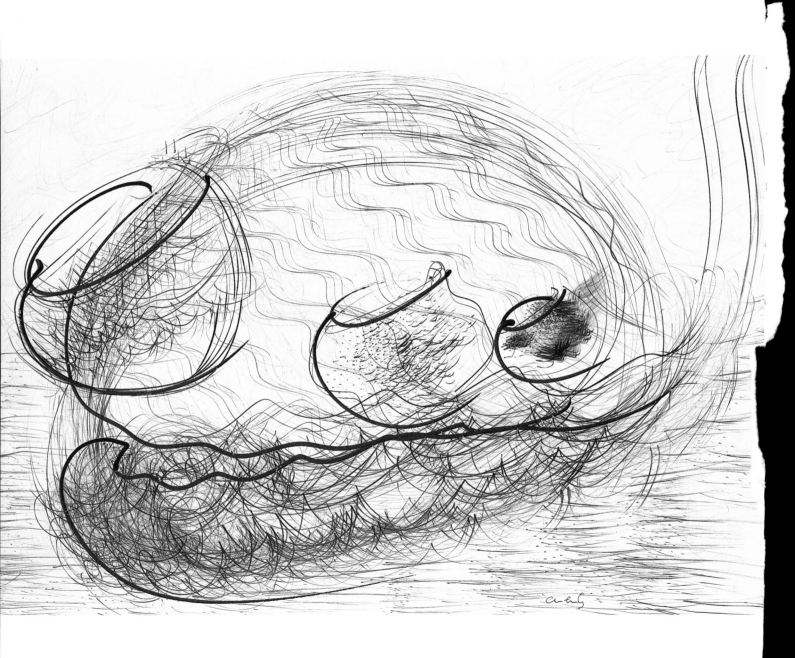

TAOS PUEBLO

Essay by Lloyd Kiva New

Governor
P.O. Box 1846
Taos, NM 87571
Ph. 505/758-9593
Fax: 505/758-4604

Government
Offices

War Chief
P.O. Box 3164
Taos, NM 87571
Ph. 505/758-3883
Fax: 505/758-2706

May 28, 1999

Dear Friends and Tribal Members:

This is a historic day for the Pueblo of Taos. It is a day when friends and neighbors come together to share the blessings of a dream brought to reality by our relatives and good friends.

We, as the Governor and the WarChief for the Pueblo of Taos, welcome you to the "Taos Pueblo Exhibition." We invite you to witness the vision of beauty and hard work for the benefit of our Young People and our Elders.

The "Taos Pueblo Exhibition" is the beginning of an exploration of the wonders of glass art. We began this trail of beauty with a guide, Dale Chihuly, who has made this art his life. He is a visionary who along with others has made it possible to share this wonderful exhibition of glass art.

The exhibition will launch the "Pueblo of Taos *Hilltop Artists in Residence*" glassblowing project which is a joint venture between the Pueblo of Taos and the Hilltop Project. This will be the birth of a dream dedicated to give all Young People, who are in need of assistance to achieve their own life goals. This is the essence of the "Glass blowing project".

It is with these good thoughts and warm feelings that we welcome the *Hilltop Artists in Residence Project* to the Pueblo of Taos. At this time, we would like to *Thank* the people of Taos Pueblo and friends for their support in this very worthwhile cause.

Sincerely,

Carl N. Concha,
Governor

Nelson J. Cordova,
WarChief

DALE CHIHULY AND THE INDIAN CONNECTION

Lloyd Kiva New

Dale Chihuly made his first trip to the Southwest in 1974, when he voluntarily veered away from his berth as the imminent head of the Glass Arts Department at the Rhode Island School of Design to accept my invitation to set up a hotshop in an old 1890s barn on the campus of the Institute of American Indian Arts (IAIA) in Santa Fe. There he would introduce glassblowing to a small group of Indian students. He was aware of but not deterred by the fact that he was about to introduce a radically different form of art and technology into a stream of Native American art/craft traditions going back thousands of years.

Interest diminished among the students following that exciting introductory session but did not die. Spores of interest in glassblowing lay dormant in the walls of the Old Barn for years, and began to fluoresce a few student generations later in the mind and hands of a singular Pueblo student graduate.

Looking back some twenty-five years to those times, I have often wondered why young Chihuly, whose illustrious career was already well under way, would voluntarily give up his time and energy to engage in this experimental teaching venture in Santa Fe.

Was it Kismet? Or was there some mysterious pull between this opportunity to work with young Indians and some unconsummated feelings about nature left over from a childhood spent on long walks by the sea and wandering through rainy Tacoma forests filled with the ghosts of an ancient Northwest Indian culture?

Who can tell? But we do know that his world and that of Indians have come together more than once in his "wildly wonderful" rise to the pinnacle of international success as a peripatetic glass artist. We also know that he likes to install his finished works in natural settings, as though not to do so would leave his statements incomplete: glass *Seaforms* shown underwater; huge icicle chandeliers set on boulders and left there to sparkle in the summer sun or freeze in winter snows; and oversized glass *Macchia* strewn like giant flowers across grassy lawns.

It is as if the creative act for him is not enough—it must be in context with the oneness and time flow of nature. Early on, he set colored neon tubes in blocks of melting ice; glass balls were thrown into rivers to float away; colored wheels of glass were mounted to catch the sunlit sky; tipi, stick, and animal forms were placed in the woods and abandoned to the elements like ancient totem poles.

In 1975, the year after his trip to Santa Fe, Chihuly was deeply and directly affected by a collection of Navajo blankets that he discovered in a museum collection. He was compelled to divert his mind and studio resources to the development of a very significant collection of simply shaped glass cylinders decorated with blanket designs. The *Navajo Blanket Cylinders* are notable in the lexicon of glass art for their unusual surface textures, and their inspired patch designs, ingeniously created by composing bits and threads of colored glass on a flat surface and then picking them up by rolling molten glass cylinders over them. The finished designs appear as softly fused multicolored vignettes of Navajo blankets. In some instances, these designs were expanded to hug the entire cylinder. Often the texture of the woven blankets is portrayed through emphasis on artistic interplay of richly colored warp and weft threads, with an occasional overlay of finely drawn colored yarns floating about like a weaver's unruly hair.

The concept of formal cylinders was expanded later to include irregularly shaped forms, to be categorized as soft cylinders. The beauty of both the straight cylinders and the soft ones lies in their creamy surface textures and the way fluidly applied colors appear to permeate them, sinking into the ivory glass surface like ink on blotter paper. The soft cylinders' walls are more flamboyantly decorated than those of the blanket series. Their undulating walls serve as a receptive surface for a suffusion of brilliant colors worked into miniature abstract paintings, which spread around the entire cylinder. These stable, thick-walled, semiopaque cylinders of either series come as close to container vessels as Chihuly ever gets. As such, they contrast sharply in concept with the fragile, transparent free forms so ubiquitously employed by him throughout the larger body of his renowned work.

The Indian connection showed up again in an even more poignant way in 1977, when Chihuly responded to a pile of nested, misshapen old Northwest Coast baskets that he happened upon at the Washington State Historical Society Museum. The inspiration gained from this serendipitous encounter led to his invention of the oversized, free form baskets that are now associated with the Chihuly look in glass art. These revolutionized the five-thousand-year-old world history of the art of glassmaking. The concept of nesting one or more glass forms into another, in often precarious groupings, constitutes a unique approach to the exhibition of glass. This is now acknowledged as another facet of Chihuly's genius. Such basket forms and their modifications underlie many of the other forms in the Chihuly repertoire.

A recent development indicates that the circle of Chihuly's involvement with Indians, which began with his 1974 visit to Santa Fe, has not yet closed. A connecting thread linked to that early IAIA venture has been carried forward through the intervening years by a singular graduate, Tony Jojola, of Isleta Pueblo. Tony's persistence and his commitment to the glassblowing discipline following those seminal days in the Old Barn eventually carried him to the doors of the Pilchuck Glass School north of Seattle, which Chihuly had cofounded. There he rejoined the world of Chihuly, glass master.

Largely through Tony's suggestion, Chihuly's blessings and support, and that of the management team of the Tacoma Hilltop Artists in Residence school of glassblowing, the circle continues. The Governing Council of the Taos Indian Pueblo has recently announced the imminent opening of a major glassblowing studio on the outlying lands of the Pueblo.

Welcome home, Dale Chihuly!

Lloyd Kiva New
President Emeritus, Institute of American Indian Arts

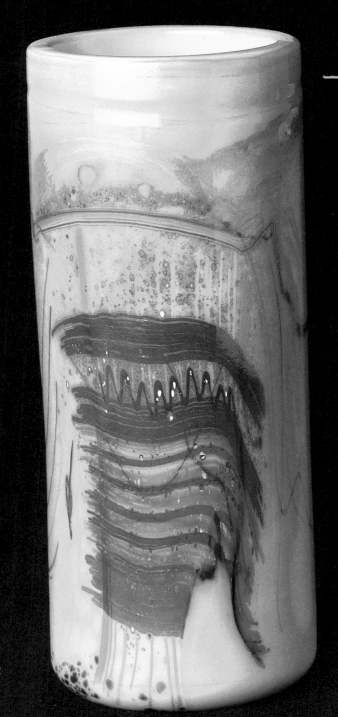
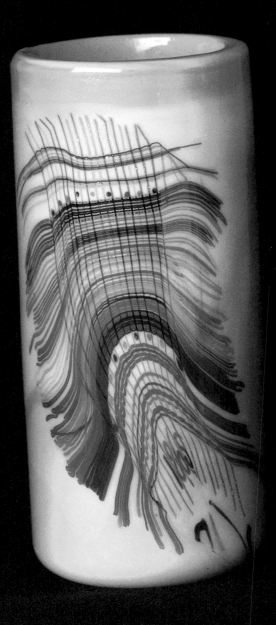

Opening Page
Cadmium Red Blanket Window, 1977, 38" x 40"

Page 6
Working Drawing #326, 1983, watercolor and graphite, 22" x 30"

Page 14
Blanket Cylinder Group, 1975

Opposite
Basket with Drawing, 1978, 11" x 8" x 7"

18

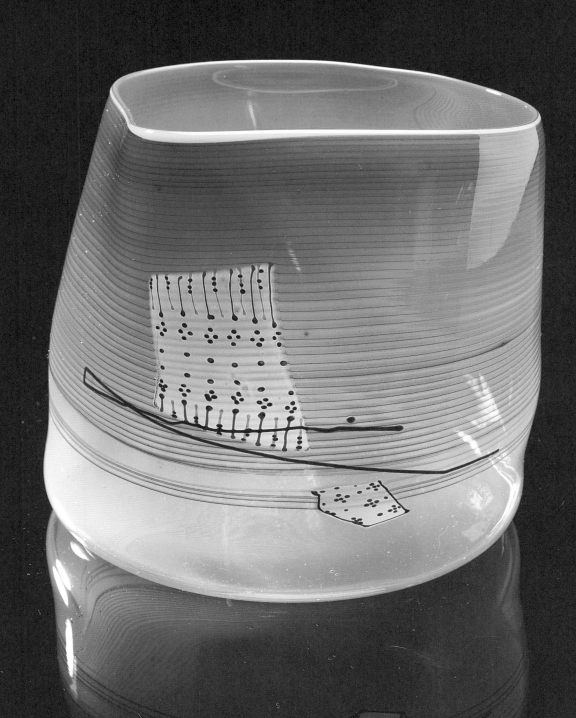

30

Page 30
Zig Zag Warp and Weft, 1978, 9" x 7" x 7"

Page 31
Four Childrens' Blankets, 1984, 18" x 10" x 10"

Opposite
Full Wrap Pueblo Cylinder, 1975, 10" x 8" x 8"

34

Page 34
Animal in Snow, 1975, 13" x 6" x 6"

Page 35
Two Horses Jumping, 1976, 15" x 8" x 8"

Opposite
Working Drawing #272, watercolor and graphite, 1980, 22" x 28"

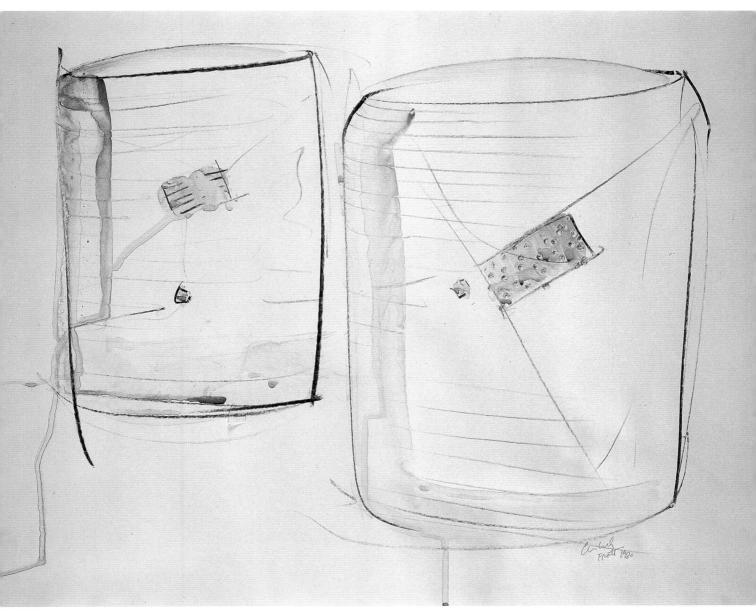

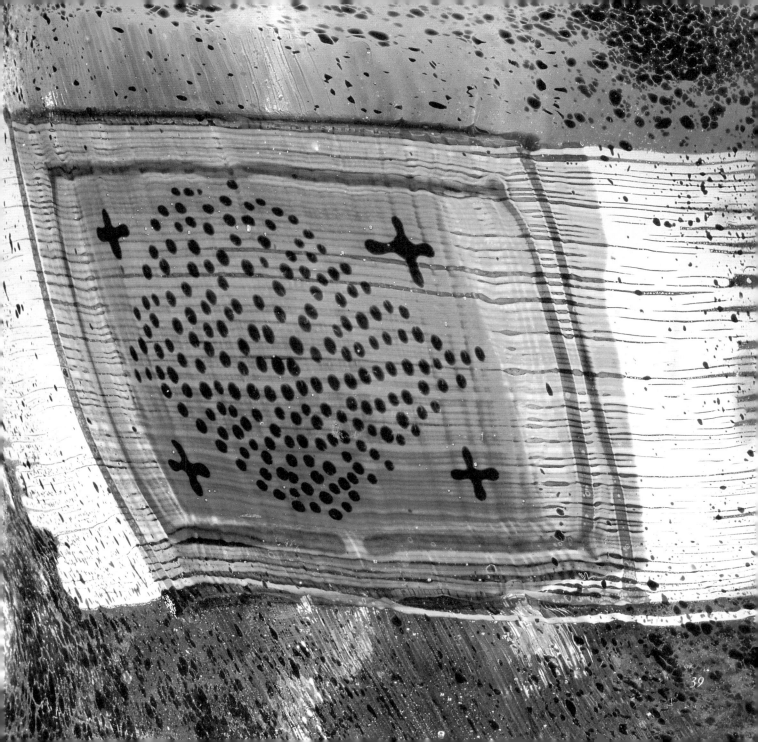

Page 38, 39
Navajo Blanket Cylinder, 1984, 12" x 7" x 7"

Opposite
Twelve Cross Cylinder, 1976, 12" x 5"

Page 48
Cylinder Group, 1995

Opposite
Winter Wisp, 1977, 8" x 9" x 9"

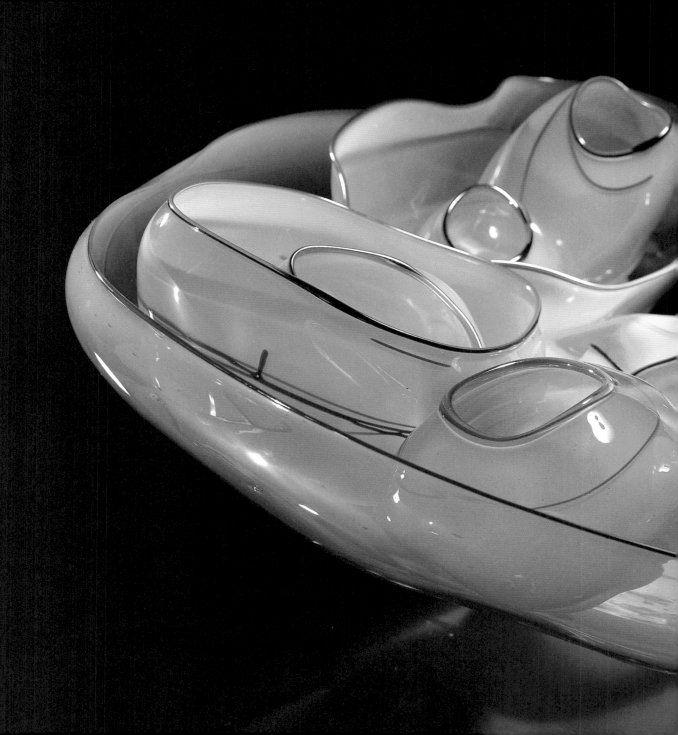

Page 52
Tabac Baskets, 1980, 7" x 17" x 18"

Opposite
Working Drawing #301, 1982, watercolor, graphite, and colored pencil, 22" x 30"

55

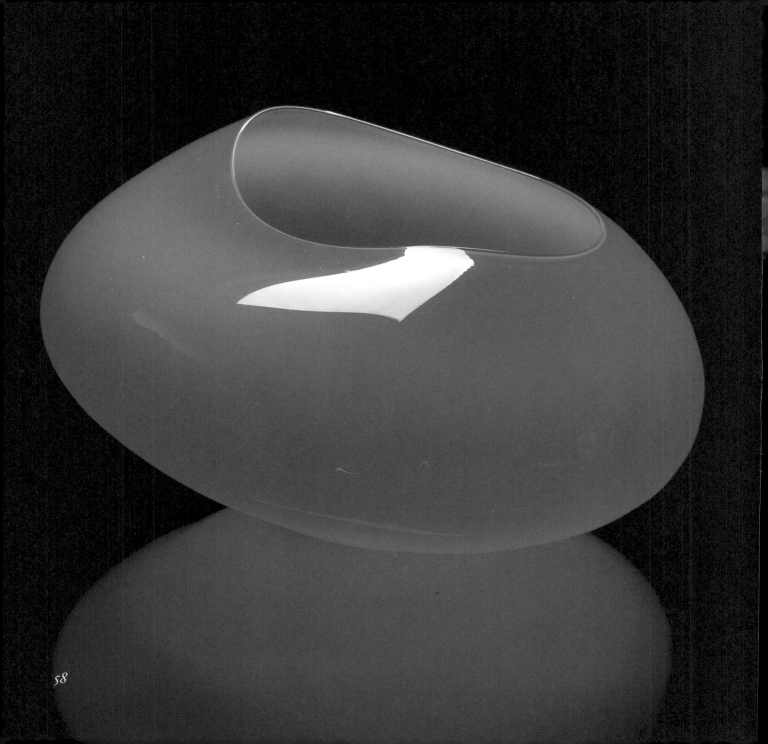

58

Page 56
Basket Group, 1993-1996

Page 58
Larkspur Blue Basket with Blue Lip Wrap, 1994, 8" x 15" x 14"

Page 59
Yellow Basket Set with Oxblood Lip Wraps, 1988, 14" x 18" x 17"

Opposite
Working Drawing #625, 1989, watercolor, ink, and graphite, 22" x 30"

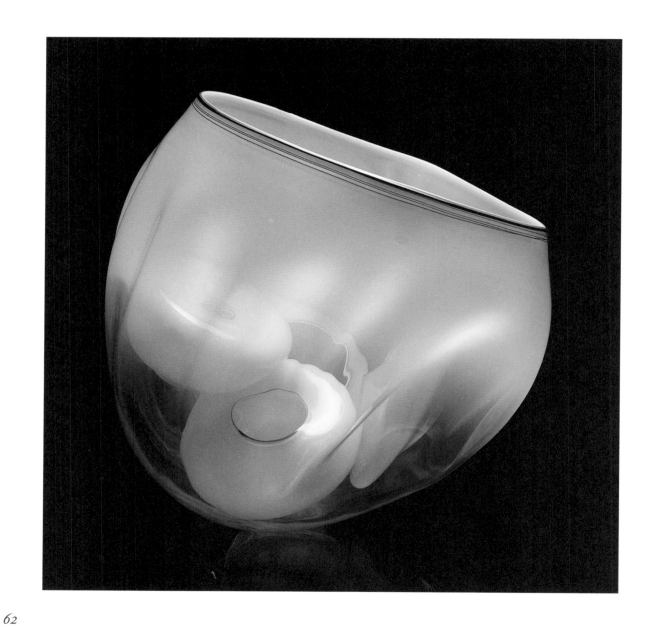

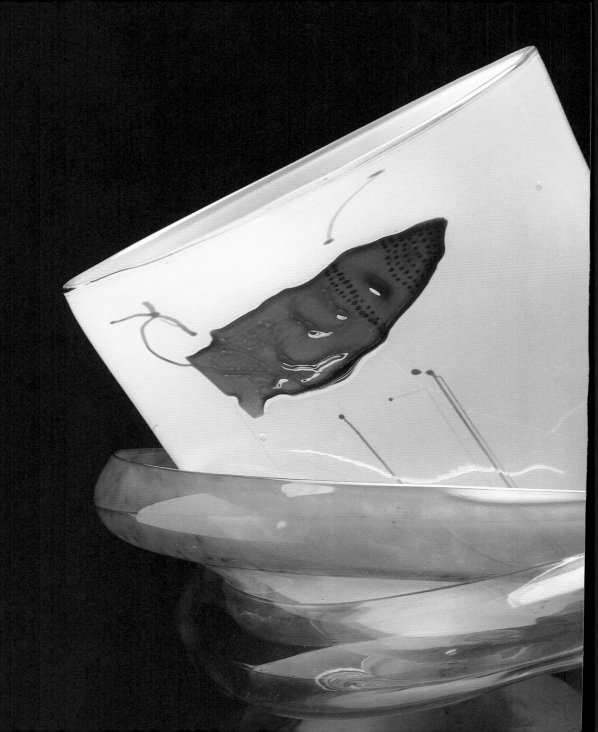

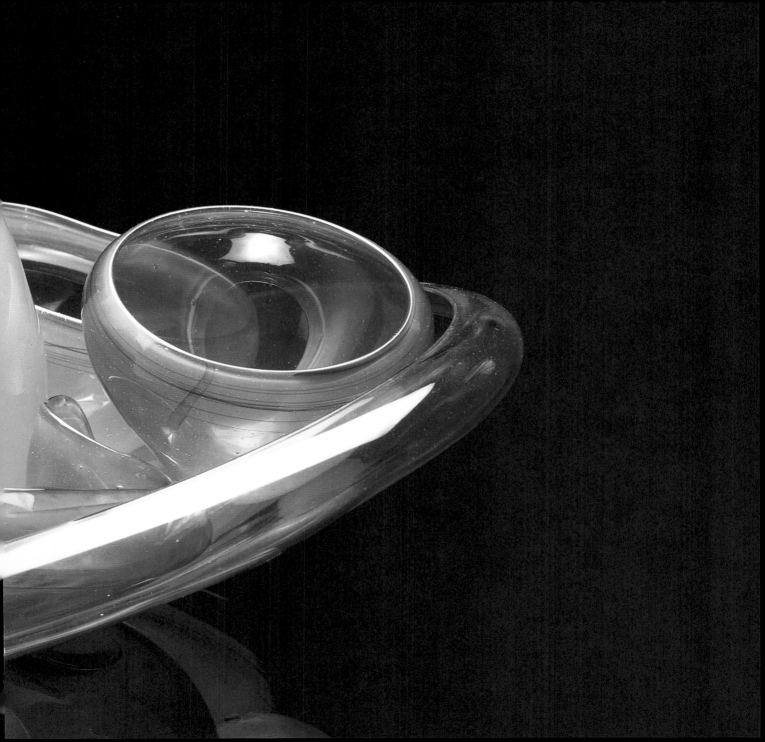

Page 62
Apple Green Basket Set with Black Lip Wraps, 1997, 21" x 16" x 17"

Page 63
Chrysanthemum Basket Set with Carbon Lip Wraps, 1993, 15" x 24" x 22"

Page 64
Transparent Amber Basket Set, 1981, 9" x 13" x 13"

Opposite
Working Drawing #317, 1983, watercolor and colored pencil, 30" x 22"

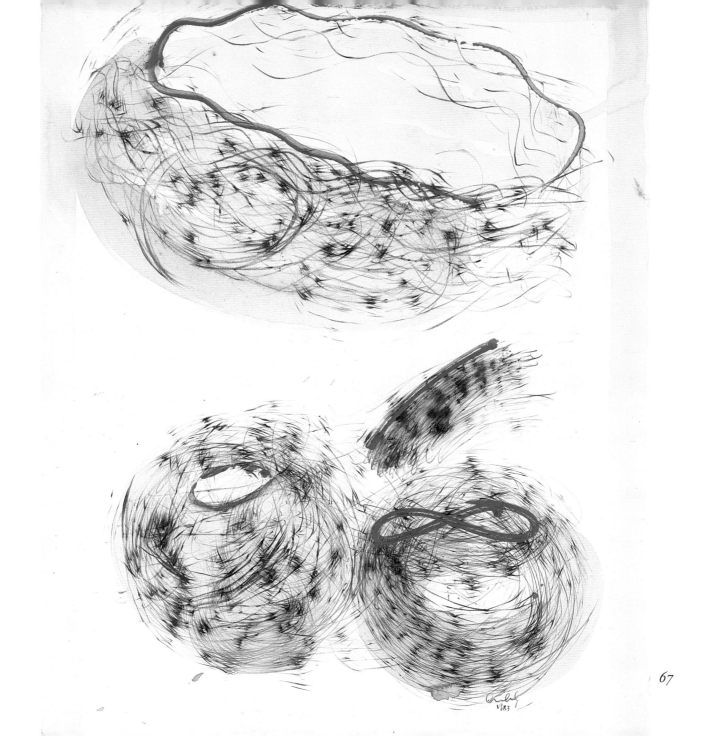

67

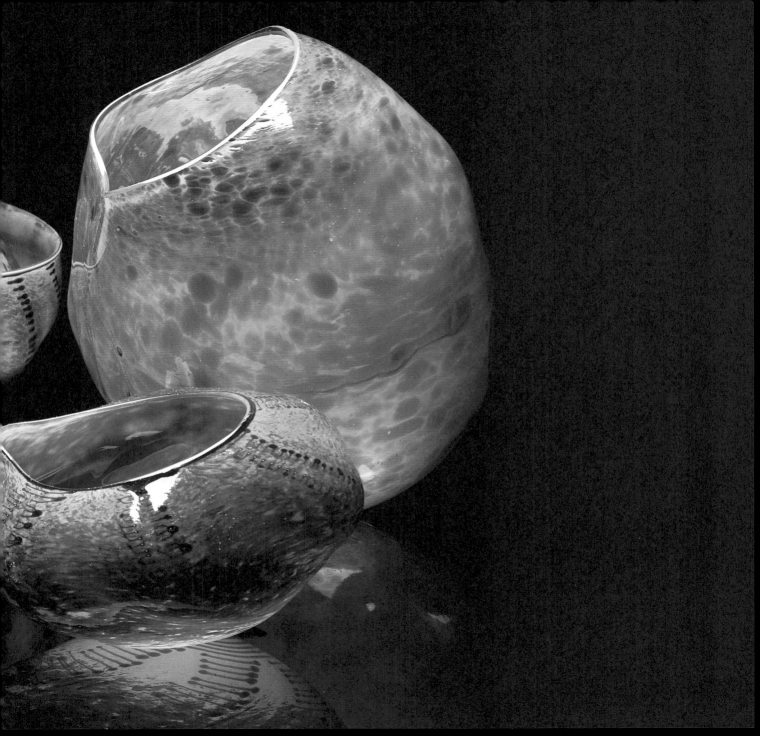

Page 68
Leopard Basket Set with Chrome Orange Lip Wraps, 1993, 6" x 24" x 22"

Page 69
Latten Yellow Basket Set with Oxblood Lip Wraps, 1993, 18" x 17" x 17"

Page 70
Early Baskets/Macchia, 1978-1980

Opposite
Working Drawing #4588, 1999, acrylic, 60" x 40"

73

Page 74
Terracotta Basket Set with Jade Green Lip Wraps, 1978, 10" x 16" x 16"

Page 75
Sepia Basket with Birch Black Lip Wrap, 1979, 10" x 9" x 9"

Opposite
Russet Brown Basket Set with Ironwood Lip Wraps, 1980, 9" x 16" x 11"

78

Page 78, 79
Working Diptych Drawing #2521, 1998, fire, acrylic, and watercolor, 42" x 60"

Page 80, 81
Working Diptych Drawing #4589, 1999, acrylic, 60" x 80"

Opposite
Rose Doré Soft Cylinder with Chartreuse Drawing, 1986, 17" x 14" x 13"

Page 84, 85
Delta Yellow Soft Cylinder with Red Ochre Drawing, 1986, 14" x 12" x 10"

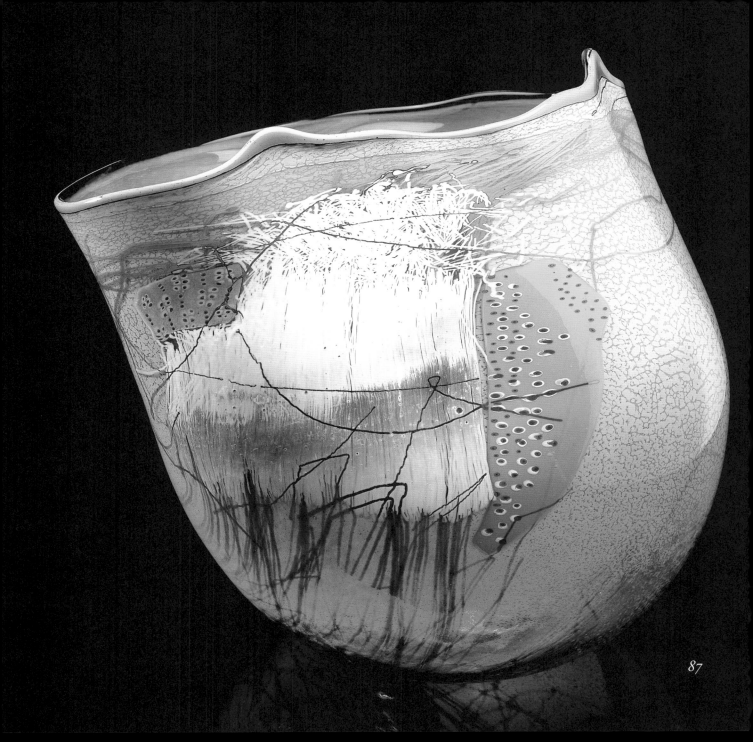

88

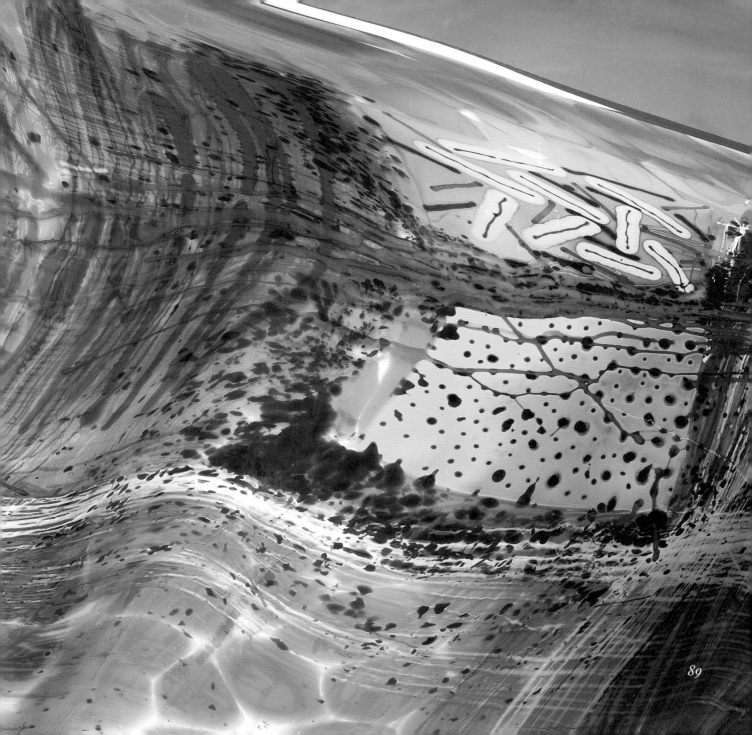

89

Page 86
Salmon Soft Cylinder with Lemon Yellow Lip Wrap, 1994, 12" x 12" x 11"

Page 87
Prussian Blue Soft Cylinder with Rose Drawings, 1988, 12" x 12" x 8"

Page 88, 89
Turquoise Green Soft Cylinder with Ochre Drawing, 1988, 17" x 17" x 14"

Opposite
Prussian Red Soft Cylinder with Blue Lip Wrap, 1992, 19" x 16" x 15"

Page 92
Soft Cylinder Group, 1992

Colophon

This first edition of *Chihuly Taos Pueblo* is limited
to 10,000 casebound copies.
The entire contents are copyright © Dale Chihuly 1999.
All Rights Reserved
Photographs by Theresa Batty, G. Dwiggins, Ira Garber,
Claire Garoutte, Scott Mitchell Leen, Teresa Rishel,
Terry Rishel, Chuck Taylor, Rob Vinnedge, and Rob Wentworth
Design by Anna Katherine Curfman
The typefaces are Garamond and Univers
Printed and bound in China by Palace Press International

Portland Press
P.O. Box 45010
Seattle, Washington 98143
800·574·7272
www.portlandpress.net

ISBN 1-57684-012-3

This book is dedicated to the future of the
TAOS PUEBLO
love
Chihly

Photograph by Geff Hinds, The News Tribune